UPBEAT DOWNBEAT BASIC CONDUCTING PATTERNS AND TECHNIQUES

Sandra Willetts

Abingdon Press
Nashville

UPBEAT DOWNBEAT
Basic Conducting Patterns and Techniques

Copyright © 1993 by Abingdon Press

This book is printed on acid-free, recycled paper.

Willetts, Sandra, 1943–
    Upbeat downbeat : basic conducting patterns and techniques / Sandra Willetts.
      p.   cm.
    ISBN 0-687-43191-3
    1. Choral conducting. 2. Church music—Instruction and study. I. Title.
    MT85.W59 1993
    782.5'145—dc20
                                                  93-8284
                                                    CIP
                                                     MN

For the information of the reader, the contents of *Upbeat Downbeat* have been closely coordinated with the contents of a videotape entitled: *Conducting: The Physical Technique: Practical Exercises for the Conductor,* also by Dr. Willetts. With the exception of the section on the SEVEN pattern, the concepts and exercises are the same in both resources. The tape is available through the Cokesbury catalogue or by writing directly to Gemini Enterprises, P. O. Box 158214, Nashville, TN 37215.

Manuscript prepared by Scott Prouty.
Musical examples printed by Gary Smoke.

93 94 95 96 97 98 99 00 01 02 — 10 9 8 7 6 5 4 3 2 1

MANUFACTURED IN THE UNITED STATES OF AMERICA

To my fondly remembered
Scarritt students (1983–88)
and to my current
Alabama students,
all of whom have helped to inspire
the continual crystallization
of the teaching of
this elusive art

Contents

Introduction

Conducting is a multifaceted craft that includes ear training, vocal training, conducting techniques, rehearsal techniques, knowledge of performance practice, music theory, and music history—not to mention basic leadership and group dynamics. It can also be an art that will consume a lifetime of study and practice. Many people have skills in some of these areas, but it is the rare person who has mastered every facet of this complex craft. The scope of this book is to address only the physical skills, the one area that everyone can master relatively quickly, regardless of the skill level of any of the other facets.

If you are a singer or an instrumentalist, you may find yourself elevated to the position of conductor because you are the best musician in the group. Even if you have had no specific conducting instructions, you are actually ahead of the game. You have already mastered the most difficult and time-consuming skill—your musicianship. Treat the conducting technique as any other musical skill that requires drill and practice, and you are on your way to becoming an effective conductor.

Those of you who are already successful conductors, blessed with natural leadership and that elusive term *charisma*, may want to improve your basic conducting techniques. Your efforts will be quickly rewarded by how much faster your choir produces the musical results you want.

Chapter One:
Basic Principles

Hand Position

In the basic HAND POSITION, the palm is facing the floor. This allows the conductor the greatest control of the sound and the greatest clarity. The motion and direction of the palm are similar to working a yo-yo or dribbling a basketball.

Figure 1

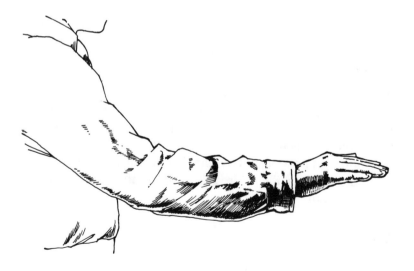

Beat (Ictus)

The moment when the open, flat palm reaches the place at which the downward direction changes to an upward direction is called the BEAT, more specifically the ICTUS, or point. It must be crisp and clear at all times. When the term *beat* refers to the entire time between two points, it is now more inclusive, and incorporates three facets: the PREP, the ICTUS, and the REBOUND. The prep is the motion before the point, and the rebound is the motion that follows it.

Staccato and Legato Articulation

The conductor can establish and/or change the articulation of the musicians by using the appropriate quality of gesture. For a STACCATO or short, detached articulation, the beat must have a sharp point and a fast rebound, as if one is touching something hot. The shorter the staccato one desires, the faster one rebounds out of the beat. This necessitates pausing at the top of the rebound so one will not fall into the next beat too quickly. For LEGATO or a smooth and flowing articulation, the beat must still be clear, but unaccented, and the rebound is slow and deliberate as if moving through water. This is not to say that the tempo is slower. The space and time of the rebound into the next beat are just more evenly distributed. If the conductor is comfortable with these two articulations, both can be adjusted by relaxing or exaggerating the rebound to achieve the desired articulation that is suggested by the actual music.

Plane of the Beat

To achieve clarity and consistency in the conducting gesture, one should be consistent with the PLANE or placement of the beats as they relate to the distance from the ground and the distance from the body. For most people (depending on individual body shapes), the distance from the ground is approximately at the curve of the elbow. This keeps the beat balanced around your center of gravity and will contribute to good breathing, and therefore good singing habits. If you have short upper arms, you may need to drop the beat slightly lower. If you are just short, stand on a podium! For those of you who conduct from the keyboard, this plane is obviously out of the question.

Figure 2

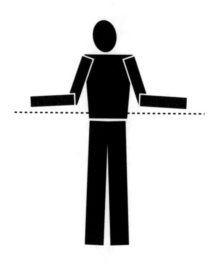

The distance from your body, again depending on individual body shapes, is approximately the length of the distance from the elbow to the hand with the upper arm slightly extended.

Figure 3

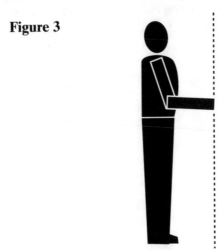

A good way to realize this plane and appreciate the consistency it can have is to sit at a keyboard and play a C major triad (C, E, G) in a 4/4 pattern.

Figure 4

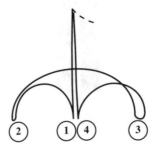

Begin at middle C for beat 1, the C below middle C for beat 2, the C above middle C for beat 3, and back to middle C for beat 4. Use the thumb for C and fingers three and five for E and G respectively.

Figure 5

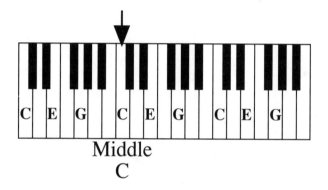

Middle
C

This exercise also helps groove the approximate distance between the beats. It does not, however, assist with the first plane, that of the distance from the ground. It will probably be too low, unless of course you have an adjustable seat and can adjust it so that the bend of your elbow is even with the keyboard. If not, try adjusting your ironing board to the desired height—assuming you remember what one looks like and/or can find it! Then place construction paper numbers at the desired spots and tap away.

Figure 6

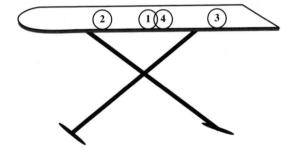

Repeated tapping at the correct height and distance is vital to grooving the proper motions. The kinetic, or muscle memory must be sufficiently trained to enable it to take over without conscious thought and/or guidance. Only when this occurs, are one's mind and ears free to deal with the myriad of musical details that will surface. One's rehearsal technique will be less than efficient or pleasant if one is struggling to remember which direction to take for beat 2 in the FOUR pattern when one should be listening to correct the B flat in the bass section. (Nothing personal men, it could have been the sopranos.)

Chapter Two:
Preparatory Gestures
and Cut-offs

Basic Principles of the Preparatory Gesture

The two most basic requirements for being a successful conductor are to be able to get your group started and eventually stopped! The level of skill one develops for these two techniques, especially the preparatory gesture, will set the tone for everything else one does as a conductor (no pun intended).

The PREPARATORY GESTURE or PREP begins just above the ictus or point of the previous beat, descends quickly to establish the place in time of that beat, and then sweeps up in a rebound, then down into the actual entry beat. ALTHOUGH EACH OF THESE MOTIONS IS IDENTIFIABLE, THEY MUST HAPPEN AS A ONE-PIECE ACTION. They constitute one beat, not two beats, not a whole measure, just one beat! A common term for this gesture is *upbeat*. Actually, this is a misnomer. While most of the motion is in fact "up," the very first and last motions are "down." One must descend to establish the point of the preceding beat as a reference to what succeeds it, and one has to get down to the actual beat.

Figure 7

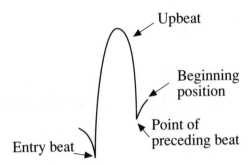

The time it takes to get from the point of the preceding beat to the point of the entry beat establishes how long it should take to get from the entry beat to the second beat. In other words, it establishes the TEMPO. The legato (smooth) or staccato (detached) style one uses in the prep establishes the style that should be used to get from the entry beat to the second beat. In other words, it establishes the ARTICULA-TION. The size and tension of the line of the prep establishes the volume at entry. In other words, it establishes the DYNAMICS. In summary, the preparatory gesture must show tempo, articulation, and dynamics.

Now the hard part! Whether one is conducting a group of instrumentalists or a group of singers, they are all going to produce sound in some manner. Except in the case of keyboards and percussion instruments, they are all going to need air or breath to activate that sound. The more breath motivating one's upbeat, the better the quality of the sound—regardless of the ability of one's group. The more advanced the group, the less they depend on the conductor for their own particular need to enhance technique. They will breathe properly regardless of your physical expertise. The less experienced group, for instance the volunteer church choir, needs the conductor to have an awesome upbeat. One must make them think they are breathing from their feet! One can do this with an aggressive and spatial prep. Let there be space in the prep for the breath and breathe with them. A word of caution here: breathe noiselessly. No audible breaths of the "vacuum cleaner" variety. If one does this in rehearsal and it becomes habitual, one is bound to do it in performance. Not a pretty sound!

Beginning on a Full Beat

Provided below are four exercises in 4/4 meter. They are designed for practicing the preparatory gesture when the music begins on a full beat, but not always on beat 1. (Where is it written that all music will begin on the first beat of the measure?) Stand motionless before beginning the prep!

Exercise 1 begins on beat 1. The beginning position will be just above the point of beat 4. Remember, descend quickly (not more than two or three inches) to establish beat 4, then swoop up and down into the entry beat, or beat 1. Remember also to breathe with your group. Begin to inhale at the point of beat 4. Practice the exercise several times, changing the articulation between legato and staccato.

Figure 8

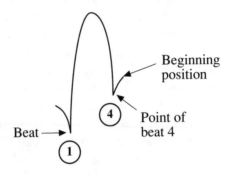

Exercise 1: Legato and Staccato

Exercise 2 begins on beat 2. The beginning position will be just above the point of beat 1. Begin to inhale at the point of beat 1.

Figure 9

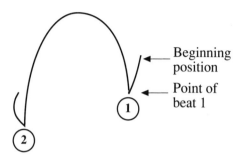

Exercise 2: Legato and Staccato

Exercise 3 begins on beat 3. The beginning position will be just above the point of beat 2. Begin to inhale at the point of beat 2.

Figure 10

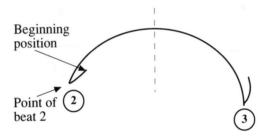

Beginning position

Point of ② beat 2

③

Exercise 3: Legato and Staccato

Exercise 4 begins on beat 4. The beginning position will be just above the point of beat 3. Begin to inhale at the point of beat 3.

Figure 11

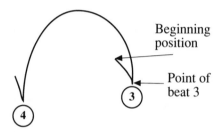

Exercise 4: Legato and Staccato

Now go back and practice these exercises again, this time experimenting with different tempi and dynamics, as well as the variety of articulations. PRACTICING IN FRONT OF A MIRROR IS VERY BENEFICIAL! And remember, you must MOTIVATE the breath to start the sound.

Beginning on a Partial Beat

Beginning on a PARTIAL BEAT is more complicated because it requires two beats of very different qualities as a prep. Two distinct pulses are necessary because the group enters on a subdivision of the beat and must have the length of the whole beat to realize its subdivision. The first of the two beats is very small, with hardly any rebound and indicates only tempo. The second of the two is much larger and very aggressive, with a sharp point and large rebound. If the first of the two beats is too large, someone will enter early. It must be a movement that elicits no active response, just information about tempo. If the second beat is not aggressive enough, the entrance will be sloppy. It must be an invitation that cannot be refused. For music that begins on the "and" of 1, the prep will be a little 4 and a big 1, with the beginning position just above the point of beat 4. Begin to inhale on the point of beat 1. It will be a short but aggressive breath.

Figure 12

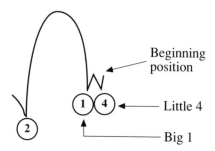

Exercise 5: Legato and Staccato

For music that begins on the "and" of 2, the prep will be a little 1 and a big 2, beginning just above the point of beat 1. Begin to inhale on the point of beat 2.

Figure 13

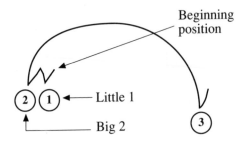

Exercise 6: Legato and Staccato

For music that begins on the "and" of 3, the prep will be a little 2 and a big 3, beginning just above the point of beat 2. Begin to inhale on the point of beat 3.

Figure 14

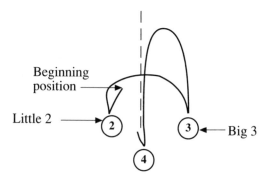

Exercise 7: Legato and Staccato

For music that begins on the "and" of beat 4, the prep will be a little 3 and a big 4, beginning just above the point of beat 3. Begin to inhale on the point of beat 4. Remember, the breath will be short but aggressive.

Figure 15

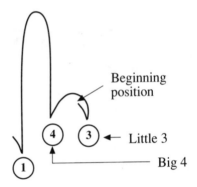

Exercise 8: Legato and Staccato

Practice these examples until you can do them with a great deal of confidence.

The Cut-off

The CUT-OFF gesture seems to be the one that develops the most personal idiosyncrasies—mostly in the form of excessive and flowery motions. Endless curlicues and pinching one's fingers together are the two most noticeable examples. Remember that we have established that the beat incorporates three facets: the PREP, the ICTUS, and the REBOUND. The cut-off also has the same facets, though in differing dimensions. The prep for the cut-off does not have to establish the previous beat since it has been well established already. Just raise the beating hand from the last beat and tap another beat followed by a small rebound with the appropriate articulation. The critical element here is that the cut-off beat must be much higher than the general beating plane or it might be misinterpreted as another beat. Also, the rebound is smaller than the regular rebound because nothing should follow it. If the music is still sounding after the rebound of one's cut-off, that will be the first clue that one's motion was less than clear. Back to the ironing board!

Go back and practice Exercises 1 through 8 again and incorporate the cut-off gesture at the end of each exercise.

Chapter Three:
Basic Patterns

Clarity is the number one priority in conducting. Equally important, however, is to be musically accurate. If what one does is clear and musically sound, the benefits of conducting are many for both you and your group.

Clear patterns will start you on the right track. Remember the two planes discussed in chapter 1. These apply across the board (not ironing) and should be maintained unless there is a musical reason to exaggerate in one direction or another.

The downbeat for each pattern should be positioned down the center of the right side of the torso. In this manner, the beating patterns can be achieved with the most comfort and clarity.

A word to the "lefties": If you are ambidextrous, use your right hand for the beat patterns. If not, go ahead and use your left hand and reverse all the directional instructions. (You should be used to that by now.) It has been my experience that the left hand dominates anyway, so you might as well use it correctly.

The ONE Pattern

The ONE pattern is just the basic straight up-and-down gesture.

Figure 16

Sometimes, if the music inspires it, the motion can become circular. Actually, it is more oval than circular. The direction should be clockwise, and there should be a definite point at the bottom.

Figure 17

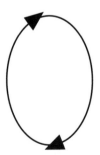

The TWO Pattern

The basic pattern is a backward *J*.

Figure 18

Notice that the point of both beats is in the same place. This works best for a legato articulation. The pattern becomes more geometric for a staccato articulation and resembles a backward and more upright check mark.

Figure 19

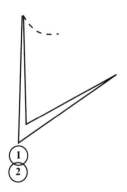

A critical element here is to keep the height of the two rebounds at the appropriate level. The rebound of beat 1 is the shorter of the two, while the rebound of beat 2 is the larger. In fact, whatever the meter, the beat that precedes beat 1 is the largest so as to forecast the downbeat. A common fault with the TWO pattern occurs when both rebounds become the same height and too close together. It all begins to look like downbeats. Be careful to keep the rebound of 1 smaller and far enough to the right to keep beat 2 distinguishable from beat 1.

Exercise 9: Legato and Staccato

The THREE Pattern

Figure 20

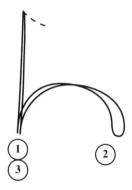

Notice that beats 1 and 3 are almost in the same place. Keep all rebounds lower than the one that precedes the down-beat, in this case, beat 3.

Exercise 10: Legato and Staccato

The FOUR Pattern

Figure 21

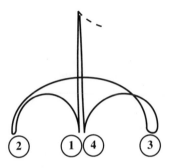

Notice that beats 1 and 4 are now in almost the same place, that beats 2 and 3 are approximately equidistant from beat 1, and that the rebound of beat 4 has the highest rebound.

Exercise 11: Legato and Staccato

The FIVE Pattern

Figure 22

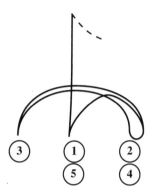

Beats 1 and 5 are now in almost the same place as are beats 2 and 4, beats 3 and 2 (4) are equidistant from beat 1, and beat 5 has the highest rebound.

Exercise 12: Legato and Staccato

This FIVE pattern is my personal favorite of the many that exist. It is not, however, the most widely used. A combination of 2 and 3 has been the most traditional.

Figure 23

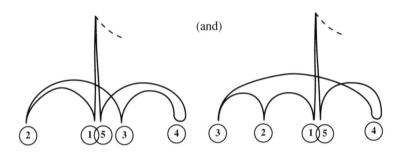

Notice that in these combinations you have to choose the appropriate pattern to match the phrasing of the music. If the phrase changes, the pattern must change. When one conducts with the second beat always going to the right, one does not have to change the pattern with the phrase. Five is five regardless of the musical phrase. One can phrase within the pattern, but the pattern does not have to change. At the same time, the motion of 2 always going to the right creates the biggest problem in learning or "grooving" this pattern. Most patterns higher than the THREE pattern have beat 2 going to the left. It will seem awkward until one gets used to it. Longer "groove time" will be necessary, but the overall consistency will be worth the extra effort. (Conducting 5/8 is another matter that will be discussed in chapter 5.)

The SIX Pattern

Figure 24

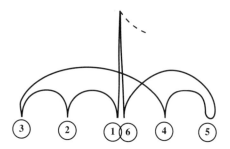

Beats 1 and 6 are now in almost the same place, beats 2 and 4 are equidistant from beat 1, as are beats 3 and 5, and beat 6 has the highest rebound.

Exercise 13: Legato and Staccato

Be aware that when a pattern has this many actual beats, they are not all equally active. In the SIX pattern, beats 1 and 4 are the strongest with beats 2, 3, 5, and 6 being weaker, or less active. Sing "Silent Night, Holy Night" and beat the SIX pattern as you sing. Make sure that your pattern reflects the concept of strong and weak, or active and inactive, beats. (Often, if the tempo is fast enough, 6/8 will be conducted in a TWO pattern.)

The Subdivided Patterns: SEVEN, NINE, and TWELVE

The next three patterns all come under the category of sub-divided patterns. The SEVEN pattern is most efficiently conducted in a basic THREE pattern with one of the basic beats getting three subdivisions, while the other two get two subdivisions. The NINE pattern is also a THREE pattern with each beat getting three subdivisions. The TWELVE pattern is a FOUR pattern with each beat getting three subdivisions.

When subdividing a basic beat by two, the rebound of the first of the two pulses must be very small, and the rebound of the second beat must be larger. The second beat's rebound is the one that transports you to the next big beat. If the subdivision is by three, the first two rebounds must be small with the third being largest. In other words, ONLY THE PULSE THAT PROPELS YOU TO THE NEXT BASIC BEAT HAS AN ACTIVE REBOUND. The point of each small beat should be in the same place as its primary beat. Regrooving the subdivided beats in that same space will keep the pattern from looking "busy" and will help maintain a steady tempo. (Note that in the figures that follow, the plus sign indicates the divided beat, which is designated as "and" in the text.)

The SEVEN Pattern

Most SEVEN patterns are some combination of two 2s and one 3: 2+2+3, 2+3+2 or 3+2+2. Therefore, this basic THREE pattern has three variations, the choice of which will be dictated by the musical phrase.

Figure 25

Variation 1   Variation 2   Variation 3

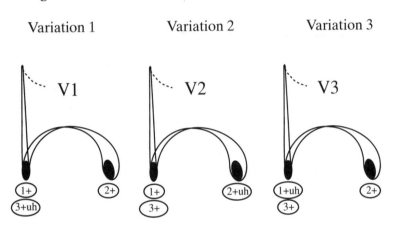

Variation 1 has that "extra" seventh beat in the third basic beat, indicating the phrase to be 2+2+3. Beats 1, 2, 5, 6, and 7 are all in the same place, beats 3 and 4 have their place and beat 7 has the highest rebound. Variation 2 shows 2+3+2, which places 1, 2, 6, and 7 in the same place, beats 3, 4, and 5 in their place and again 7 has the highest rebound. Variation 3 shows 3+2+2 with beats 1, 2, 3, 6, and 7 in the same place, beats 4 and 5 in their place and beat 7 having the highest rebound. It is worth reminding you once again to beat the inactive and active beats appropriately.

Exercise 14*a*: Legato and Staccato (use Variation 1)

Exercise 14*b*: Legato and Staccato (use Variation 2)

Exercise 14*c*: Legato and Staccato (use Variation 3)

The NINE Pattern

Figure 26

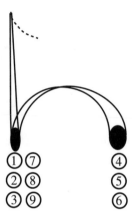

The NINE pattern is simply a THREE pattern with each beat subdivided by three. Beats 1, 2, 3, 7, 8, and 9 are all in the same place, beats 4, 5, and 6 have their place and beat 9 has the highest rebound. Again, keep the active and inactive beats distinguishable.

Exercise 15: Legato and Staccato

The TWELVE Pattern

Figure 27

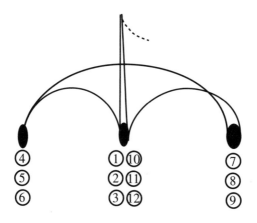

The TWELVE pattern is simply a FOUR pattern with each beat subdivided by three. Beats 1, 2, 3, 10, 11, and 12 are all in the same place, 4, 5, and 6 have their place, as do 7, 8, and 9. Beat 12 has the highest rebound. The same encouragement about active and inactive beats applies.

Exercise 16: Legato and Staccato

Chapter Four: Subdividing Appropriate Patterns

Y ou have already become familiar with the basic princi-
ples of subdividing in the previous chapter. When conducting music written in 2/2, 3/2, and 4/2 at a tempo
slow enough to require a pulse on each quarter note, the appropriate pattern should be used. The same principle applies when
conducting music written in 2/4, 3/4, and 4/4 and an eighth note
pulse is desired.

The TWO-TWO Pattern

One should beat 2/2 with a subdivided TWO pattern and not a FOUR pattern. This renders all of the beats to be basically in the same place only to be delineated by clear rebounds. The "and" of 2 will have the highest rebound. Remember that only the pulse that propels you to the next basic beat has an active rebound.

Figure 28

Exercise 17: Legato and Staccato

The THREE-TWO Pattern

Beat the 3/2 pattern with a subdivided THREE pattern and not a SIX pattern. If the SIX pattern is used, the accents will be on 1 and 4 instead of 1, 2, and 3. This divides the measure in half rather than thirds. Using a subdivided THREE pattern renders beats 1 "and," and 3 "and" in the same place, with 2 "and" in its place. The "and" of 3 has the highest rebound.

Figure 29

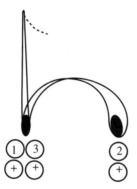

Exercise 18: Legato and Staccato

The FOUR-TWO Pattern

Beat the 4/2 pattern with a subdivided FOUR pattern. This renders beats 1 "and," and 4 "and" in the same place with beats 2 "and" and 3 "and" in their respective places. The "and" of 4 has the highest rebound. Also notice that beats 2 and "and" are equidistant from 1, as are beats 3 and "and," just like the basic FOUR pattern.

Figure 30

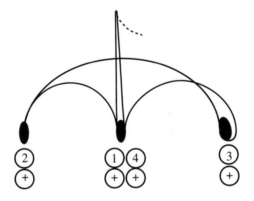

Exercise 19: Legato and Staccato

Chapter Five:
Odd Meters in a Fast Tempo

The FIVE Pattern

W hen odd meters are in a fast tempo, it is more efficient to beat them in fewer beats. For instance, 5/8 works best as a basic TWO pattern with one of the beats incorporating the space and time necessary for that extra eighth note. The phrase will most likely be 2+3 or 3+2, and which variation to use will be dictated by the musical phrase.

Figure 31

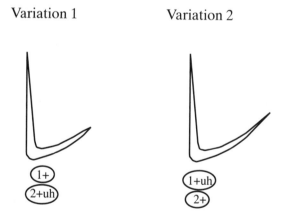

Variation 1   Variation 2

The critical issue here is to show the extra time in the beat by adding extra space. The expression "hang time" is helpful in trying to identify the length of the elongated beat. The tendency will be to start back in or down too soon. Count aloud as you beat variation 2: "1 and uh 2 and." Continue the outward motion until you have completely finished counting the first full beat (i.e., "1 and uh"). Do the same with the shorter beat. The feeling of continual movement away from the beat or a slightly suspended feeling at the top of the beat is called "hang time."

Exercise 20: Legato and Staccato (use Variation 1)

Exercise 21: Legato and Staccato (use Variation 2)

Exercise 22: Legato and Staccato (use Variation 1 for two bars, then Variation 2 for two bars)

Exercise 23: Legato and Staccato (begin with Variation 1, then alternate in each bar)

The SEVEN Pattern

For 7/8, all the same information applies except that now the basic pattern is a THREE pattern with one of the beats being elongated in space and time for that extra eighth note. The phrase will most likely be 3+2+2, 2+3+2 or 2+2+3, and which variation to use will be dictated by the musical phrase.

Figure 32

Variation 1   Variation 2   Variation 3

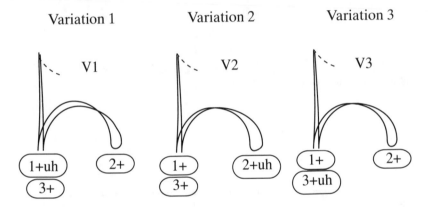

It is good practice to count aloud as you rehearse these exercises. The added involvement of other senses deepens the "groove" time and enhances the learning process greatly.

Exercise 24: Legato and Staccato (3+2+2) (1 and uh 2 and 3 and). Use Variation 1.

Exercise 25: Legato and Staccato (2+3+2) (1 and 2 and uh 3 and). Use Variation 2.

Exercise 26: Legato and Staccato (2+2+3) (1 and 2 and 3 and uh). Use Variation 3.

Exercise 27: Legato and Staccato (use Variation 1 for two bars, Variation 2 for two bars, then Variation 3 for two bars)

Exercise 28: Legato and Staccato (use Variations 1, 2, and 3 respectively, then repeat)

Practice these exercises slowly but steadily at first, then gradually increase the tempo. Remember to count aloud and also use a metronome. Try ♩ = 120 at first. You'll find that it will not take you long to get to ♩ = 200+. In fact, it is easier at a faster tempo. The critical issue here, as it is for all conducting, is to MAINTAIN A STEADY TEMPO. If you can conduct odd meters clearly and in tempo, you can conduct anything and with confidence! Remember that only practice will build the techniques, and only when you are comfortable with the techniques will you be confident.

Chapter Six:
Frequent Meter Changes

There is much music available that utilizes mixed meters. That is to say, the musical phrase dictates the need for more than one meter in the same piece. When the meter changes, something will remain constant, either the basic BEATING UNIT or a particular NOTE VALUE. Sometimes they are one and the same, sometimes they are not. When they differ, which to keep constant is usually specified by the composer.

Beating Unit Remains Constant

For the first three exercises in this chapter, the basic BEATING UNIT, in this case, the quarter note, remains constant. Practice these until you can make easy transitions from one meter to the next. If you have "grooved" the basic patterns well enough, it becomes more of a mental feat than a physical or musical feat.

Exercise 29: Legato and Staccato

Exercise 30: Legato and Staccato

Exercise 31: Legato and Staccato

Note Value Remains Constant

For Exercises 32, 33, and 34, the NOTE VALUE remains constant, in this case the eighth note. This means that in Exercise 32, bar 3 will be longer by two eighth notes than bars 1 and 2. Bar 5 will be one eighth note shorter than bars 1 and 2. Be sure to conduct the 6/8, 3/8, 5/8, and 7/8 bars in the smallest number of beats: 6/8 in TWO, 3/8 in ONE, 5/8 in TWO, and 7/8 in THREE. These exercises should be done at a fairly brisk pace. It would be too unwieldy to actually conduct each eighth note.

Exercise 32: Legato and Staccato

Exercise 33: Legato and Staccato

Exercise 34: Legato and Staccato

Exercise 35 is the same as Exercise 32, but with different instructions. If the BEATING UNIT remained constant, in this case the quarter note, the third and fifth bars would sound like triplets. The instructions would be ♩ = ♩. Having this concept clear in your mind and then in your hand will go a long way toward building confidence.

Exercise 35: Legato and Staccato

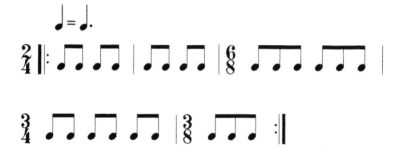

Chapter Seven:
Ritardandos and Accelerandos

Ritarding and Subdividing

When one is conducting in a certain meter and the tempo ritards (slows) enough to warrant controlling the inner beats, one must SUBDIVIDE. The same techniques for subdivision as discussed in chapters 3 and 4 apply here. The first of the two beats must be small. Only the beat that propels one into the next basic beat is large. As you practice these exercises, be sure the tempo ritards enough for the need to subdivide.

Exercise 36: Legato

Exercise 37: Legato

Exercise 38 could require a third subdivision. If the tempo is very slow and more than one singer or player is executing the sixteenth note, you may prefer to dictate that note. Be careful that the subdivisions just ahead of it are small enough not to elicit that sixteenth note too soon.

Exercise 38: Legato

Accelerating and Merging

When one is conducting in a large numbered meter and the tempo accelerates to the point where that meter becomes inefficient, MERGE into a smaller numbered pattern. It must be done with tremendous conviction and aggressiveness. The moment of change from one meter to the next must be exaggerated and immediately clear.

Exercise 39: Staccato (begin in SIX, then merge into TWO)

Exercise 40: Staccato (begin in THREE, then merge into ONE)

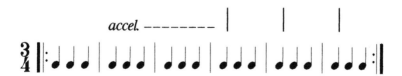

The aggressiveness with which you must execute the ritard and the acceleration cannot be underplayed. You must lead out with conviction and authority. Slowing a large group and maintaining the ensemble (rhythmic togetherness) is sometimes like slowing a Mack truck. They tend to speed up on their own—though never quite together! You must be in control, whatever the musical demand.

Chapter Eight:
Miscellaneous Techniques

Internal Phrasing

One of the most useful and timesaving techniques in conducting is to be able to show an INTERNAL PHRASE or breath, especially when it is not obvious in the music. It is a tedious task for the conductor and the group to give all of the breathing marks verbally. If you can show them, everyone benefits. Even when you must verbally instruct, you can then continue to reinforce the instructions visually. For a breath after beat 3 in a four-beat bar, gently stop after beat 3, and then use a swooping upbeat with what appears to be a beginning prep to beat 4.

This two-piece action must show two things: that you want them to stop, and that they need a good breath to continue. The critical issue is not to let the tempo lag. Even though the two actions are of unequal proportion, the upbeat being quicker, together they must equal only one beat. It is like the adage, "Robbing Peter to pay Paul." Also, the more comfortable the technique becomes, the more it appears to be a one-piece action and becomes more of a "hint" rather than an overt action. After your group knows that they are to breathe in a particular spot, this action can be more relaxed, though not disappear entirely.

Exercise 41 indicates the breath to be after beat 3 consistently, while Exercise 42 varies the breaths. Practice Exercise 41 until the technique becomes comfortable before proceeding to Exercise 42.

Exercise 41: Legato

Exercise 42: Legato

Dynamics

This technique is perhaps the easiest of all to master. In general, the bigger the beat, the louder the sound. Conversely, the smaller the beat, the softer the sound. This is mostly true, but the amount of tension (pull) or weight in the line can also indicate the volume level. Try all three exercises using first the size variation, second, adding or subtracting tension or weight, then a combination of both. You will, in fact, encounter music that will benefit from all of the above.

A word of caution about the preparatory beat for a soft entrance. If it is too small, it will not motivate a good breath. Remember that a soft sound, whether singing or playing, requires as much, if not more breath than a loud sound. The prep must have breathing space in it. It is a question of tension or weight in that motion that will influence the volume.

Exercise 43: Legato and Staccato (*piano,* then *forte*)

Exercise 44: Legato and Staccato

Exercise 45: Legato and Staccato

Accents

Accenting notes within an already established volume and/or articulation requires abrupt and aggressive movements. The critical issue here is that this motion must function far enough ahead of the desired action to actually cause the action. To hit the designated accented note harder is not enough. The rebound from the previous beat must forecast the sudden change. Be aggressive, be dramatic! Look like the sound of the music you want!

Exercise 46: Legato and Staccato

Cueing

A common misconception about cueing is that it is completely the responsibility of the left hand. NOT true. When a cue for the section on your right comes on beat 3 in a FOUR pattern, it coincides with the beating hand. If you insist on reinforcing it with the left hand, you could look more like a hula dancer than a conductor. Just use your beating hand and reinforce with the head and eyes. If a cue is needed on beat 3 in a FOUR pattern for the section on your left, then use your left hand. Be sure to BRING IT UP IN TIME TO GIVE A PREP, then show the actual beat with its follow-through or rebound. Notice that the isolated cue has the same facets as the beat: a prep, ictus, and rebound.

For Exercise 47, imagine your choir to be seated SATB from your left respectively. That puts the basses on your right and in line for the cue on beat 3 with your beating hand. Repeat the exercise and cue the sopranos on beat 3 with your left hand.

Exercise 47: Legato and Staccato

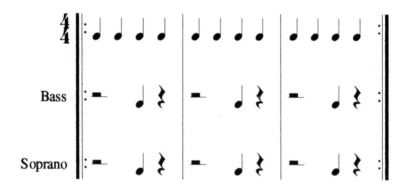

Left Hand

Independent use of the left hand is generally the last technique with which to become comfortable. Not many of us are truly ambidextrous, nor do we want to put in the practice time that would enable us to appear so. The most common fault one sees is the involuntary thumping of the beat with the left hand as it attempts to mold a legato line or influence a gradual *crescendo.*

Practice Exercise 48, hands alone at first, especially the left hand. Let it gradually rise as it extends toward the group with the palm up. Move with a considerable amount of tension in your hand and arm. For the *decrescendo,* reverse the action by drawing the hand back to your body and relaxing the tension. DO NOT TURN THE PALM OVER TOO SOON. As soon as the group sees an open palm facing them, it functions as a "STOP" sign. Do not turn the palm over completely until your hand is almost to your chest, as should be your beating hand. Then both can function together for the cut-off. The beating hand in this exercise should reinforce the dynamic action as well.

Exercise 48: Legato

To encourage independence of the left hand, may I suggest that you reread this volume and do all of the exercises with the left hand only! Remember that the patterns will have a mirror image. In a FOUR pattern with the left hand, beat 2 will go to your right. In a THREE pattern, beat 2 will go to your left, and so on.

Now, the third time being the charm, use both hands on every exercise in a mirroring action. There will be times when mirroring the beating hand will be at least preferable, if not necessary. You may want to reinforce a musical idea, or your group may be very large or positioned in several locations. Their sight line may require you to use both hands. Be careful, however, to mirror the beating hand only when necessary. It can become a habit that is difficult to break.

Conclusion

Well, if you have really been through this book three times and if you have physically practiced all of the exercises, you should be well on your way to setting a good basis as a beginner, or reshaping some basic techniques as a veteran. Unfortunately there is no shortcut. The amount of physical practice or "groove time" needed to make a new technique your own, or harder yet, regrooving an old one, is immeasurable. You simply must practice until you can do it without conscious thought. As stated in the introduction, practice these techniques as you would practice techniques for any musical instrument. The benefits are limitless for both you and your group.

About the Author

In the fall of 1989, Sandra Willetts began her appointment as Director of Choral Activities at the University of Alabama. Previously, she has held positions as Professor of Conducting and Music Department Chairperson at Scarritt Graduate School in Nashville, Tennessee, and Director of Choral Activities at both Middle Tennessee State University and St. Mary's College of Maryland. Dr. Willetts has also served as Visiting Professor at the University of Iowa and Duquesne University in Pittsburgh, Pennsylvania.

Dr. Willetts has degrees from Westminster College, Indiana University, and the University of Cincinnati. Her conducting teachers include Julius Herford, Fiora Contino, Elmer Thomas, and Helmuth Rilling. She has assisted in the preparation of choruses for Leonard Bernstein (also was a member of the original cast and road company of "Mass"), Robert Shaw, and James Levine.

Listed in "Outstanding Young Women in America" for three consecutive years, Dr. Willetts was also the conductor of the Nashville Symphony Chorus and guest conductor of the Nashville Symphony Orchestra for three years. A popular clinician and guest conductor, festivals and workshops for high schools, colleges, and churches have taken her to more than twenty states and Canada.

Notes